Canadian Poems for Canadian Kids

www.frontiercollege.ca

This book is brought to you by
Frontier College and our generous supporters

FRONTIER
COLLEGE

COLLÈGE
FRONTIÈRE

Ce livre vous est gracieusement présenté par
Collège Frontière et ses généreux donateurs

www.collegefrontiere.ca

Canadian Poems for Canadian Kids

Edited by Jen Hamilton

Illustrated by Merrill Fearon

With a Foreword by P.K. Page

SUB WAY

VANCOUVER

Foreword © 2005 by P.K. Page

Library and Archives Canada Cataloguing in Publication

Canadian poems for Canadian kids/edited by Jen
Hamilton; illustrated by Merrill Fearon.

ISBN 0-9736675-0-8

1. Children's poetry, Canadian (English) 2. Canadian poetry
(English)–20th century. I. Hamilton, Jen II. Fearon, Merrill

PS8273.C24 2005   jC811'.540809282
C2005-900699-4

Subway Books Ltd.
1819 Pendrell Street, Unit 203
Vancouver, B.C. V6G 1T3 Canada
Website: *www.subwaybooks.com*
E-mail: *subway@interlog.com*

Canadian orders:
Customer Order Department
University of Toronto Press Distribution
5201 Dufferin Street
Toronto, Ontario M3H 5T8

US orders:
University of Toronto Press Distribution
2250 Military Road
Tonawanda, New York 14150
Tel: (716) 693-2768
Fax: (716) 692-7479

Toll-free ordering from Canada or the US:
Tel: 1-800-565-9523
Fax: 1-800-221-9985
Email: *utpbooks@utpress.utoronto.ca*

Contents

FOREWORD
P.K. Page

Poetry is a vitally important literary form, one too often overlooked in this age of fast food, fast facts and fast living. Who has time for it?

And yet, if *my* fast facts are correct, respectable psychologists claim that in order to develop the full powers of the mind, early exposure to metered verse is essential. Some go even further, suggesting that the reading of poetry develops pattern recognition, a sophisticated sense of time and timing and, more importantly, such positive emotions as peacefulness and love.

Put another way, we need poets and their poetry–for reasons beyond our actual enjoyment of the words. Homer and all the poets since, who have told us about ourselves, have done so in rhythms that may have been shaping our brains. Who knows what Shakespeare has done to us with his iambic pentameter?

Frederick Turner, the poet and polymath, and Ernst Pöppel, a brain researcher, both deplore the rise of what they call utilitarian education and the loss of folk poetry. The disappearance of the latter, they suggest, may lead to the success of political and economic tyranny. And "the masses, starved of the beautiful and complex rhythms of poetry, are susceptible to the brutal and simplistic rhythms of the totalitarian slogan or advertising jingle."

If I strike a serious note, it is because we live in serious times–times in which, more than ever, our children need all the help–and the joy–that poetry offers.

Stories

Irene N. Watts

At night when I can't fall asleep, I wait for
stories to enter my head.
Everything
has a story.
The wind and the mountains
stars in the sky
fierce prairie storms
passing by:
A world full of stories
filled with words
full of delight:
Words to make me wonder
Sometimes to shiver with fright.
Tales of magic:
A horse with wings
medieval palaces
of sorcerers, of kings.
Stories that can take me far
to strange and distant lands,
to hear a mermaid singing,
or dance
on silvery sands.

Stories full of monsters,
who lived so long ago,
in my dreams they tell me secrets
all I need to know.
A world full of stories
on which to grow.

Treasures

Beryl Young

Come with me to the ocean
and we will find some treasures.
We'll find rocks with rings like planets
and shells and long, white feathers.
We'll watch the sweeping seagulls,
hear the eeping calls of seals.
The waves will lick like kittens' tongues
against our sturdy heels.

A Song About Me

Patience Wheatley

It's going to rain
I'll wear my red slicker
and jump in the puddles
and splash my dog
and save worms from drowning
and make mud pies
for my sixth birthday

The sun's coming out
I'll wear my green T-shirt
and plant a flower
and sling sticks in the lake
for birds to sit on

It's cloudy again
I'm strapped in my car seat
pretending to drive
an eight-wheeler truck
behind my Dad
on our way to see Gramma

When the snow comes
I'll work with my shovel
and make a fort
with towers and windows
and a snowman with a carrot nose

and stones for eyes
and my own wooly hat
so he won't catch cold

Soon it's night
I'll sit in my cozy bath
and sail my ducks
and put on my sleepers
and rabbity slippers
and cuddle up to Mom
for a song
about me.

Allergic to Numbers

Linda Rogers

I'm allergic to numbers.
They make me feel nervous and sickly.
When the class is doing arithmetic,
my skin gets bumpy and itchy.

Some people can't eat strawberries
and cat fur gets them wheezing,
but just start talking digits to me
if you want to hear funny breathing.

Talk to me about baseball
and the figures for pitches and hits
or which number won the lottery
and my immune system quits.

I can't give you my address
or tell you what number to phone.
If you want to come over and visit,
you'll have to follow me home.

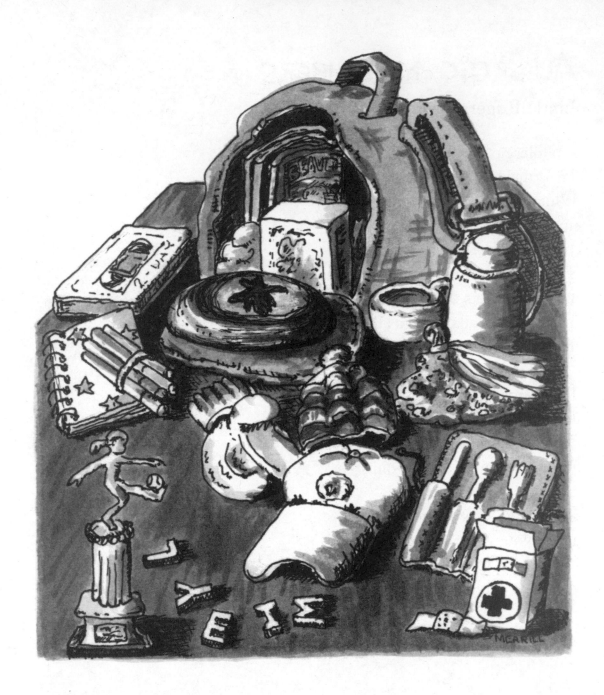

Emily's Backpack

Diane Dawber

Emily's backpack is huge, so huge
it looks as though Emily
is carrying a bear
or a small bison
or maybe a Galapagos turtle
yes, that's it—a Galapagos turtle
because once
when Emily was trying to get on the bus
the backpack was so heavy
it toppled her backward onto the sidewalk
helpless
until three big boys and the bus driver
hauled her aboard.

Once when we were studying life cycles at school
Emily opened her backpack
to find her cat had had two kittens inside.

Once when the teacher was trying to explain archeology
she excavated Emily's backpack
layer by layer

down through food and clothes
the books and pencils
until she got down to wrapping paper
Emily had made in Art Class
the Christmas before last.

If you're hungry at recess
you can always ask Emily for something to eat
as long as you don't mind backpack fuzz.

If you need socks for gym
you can always ask Emily for something to wear
as long as you don't mind red and green stripes and a musty smell.

If you want an excuse to get out of class
you can always pretend
to trip over Emily's backpack and hurt yourself
as long as you don't blame her,
"Ow! Oooh! I'm sorry Emily, I wasn't looking where I was going."

Best of all
when you have to get ready for your fitness test
you can ask Emily to let you carry her backpack for a while.

You need the exercise and she needs the break.

Beetle

Allan Serafino

A tiny fellow,
a miniature tank overturned,
so tiny I didn't notice him

with his feet grasping
for a hook of sky
to right himself again.

What a surprise
to slip on this floor
so waxy and smooth

he must have wondered
if the world had gone
mad. Maybe it did.

A tiny fellow.
I play giant to his wee
world and turn him back

on to upsidedness
for beetles, on the grass.
Who knows, maybe one day

it will be his turn
to look me in the eye,
with his giant's eye.

I'll be careful
where I step
the next time.

Choosing

Vicki Goodfellow Duke

I fill my pocket
with stones,

flat and gray,

long ones, jagged
as swords,

speckled red
from the north side
of the Moon.

I take them to my room
to hear their secrets.

Just pick one,
says Mom.
They're all the same.

But she doesn't know
about secrets
or leprechauns either.

I choose a round stone,
smooth and blue,

a tiny world

fit for a kingdom.

I keep it hidden
in a grand place

with plenty of room
for the little knight
to stretch his arms

and build castles,

one thousand colored stones
in his pocket.

Hiccups

Alison Lohans

I hate to have the hiccups.
They're something I despise.
When you least expect it,
    hic!
they catch you by surprise.

Like when you're hanging out with friends,
and feeling rather cool.
Other kids come walking by—
    hic!
They think you're such a fool!

Sometimes you give a speech in class;
you're feeling pretty wise.
Everybody's listening, then
    hic!
and tears come to your eyes.

Or say in art you're trying hard
to draw a perfect line.
You hold your breath to concentrate—
    hic!
and now you've wrecked your whole design.

You're feeling sort of shy one day
and kind of lonely, too.
You're sitting there real quietly, but
        hic!
So everybody laughs at you.

The only time they did me good
was in the dentist's chair.
That drill was grinding down my tooth, and
        hic! ...hic!
          hiccup!
The dentist didn't dare go on
and I got out of there!

But usually they make me –*hic!*–so mad.
It's always so embar–*hic!*–rassing
to hiccup right out loud,
especially when you–*hic!*–sing.
Or when your mouth is full–*hic!*–
of food–*hiccup!*
Or when you–*hic!*
you try–*hiccup!*
to tell a–*hiccup!*–no, not a
hiccup, a jo–*hic!*–
a joke, and–

hic!... hic!
HICCUP!

See what I–*hic!*–mean?

Menu from The Bug House Family Restaurant

Beverley Brenna

Instead of thinking bugs are gross
Please don't be so suspicious!
With half a chance, and one good chef
You'll find they're quite delicious!

On Monday night, the Bug House makes
Hundreds of mosquito steaks!
Each mosquito's sliced and fried
And served with spiders on the side.

On Tuesday, count on termite pie
Guaranteed to satisfy.
And for the smaller appetite,
Crispy wings are nice and light.

On Wednesday, we serve wasp soup
By the spoon or by the scoop.
Guaranteed to make you grin,
Order stinger out
Or in.

On Thursday we have Bug Surprise,
Made with centipedes and flies,
Then Bugs with Cream or A La Mode
And Buggy Breath Mints for the road.

Cooked and served beside your chair,
Fireflies are Friday's fare.
For this very special treat,
Phone ahead to save a seat.

On Saturday we lift the rugs
And boil up the carpet bugs.
Served with leggy spider wine—
A perfect way for two to dine.

Sunday night's Aerobic Night
When you can catch your food in flight.
Put your muscles to the test,
It's active dining at its best!

When Grandpa Gets to Fiddling

Robin Patterson

When Grandpa lifts his violin
And props it 'neath his chin,
I can hardly hold my horses
For the dancing to begin.

My fingers snap, my knuckles knock,
My toes begin to tap.
My shoulders shrug, my elbows bend,
My hands begin to clap.

And very soon I'm whirling, twirling,
Jumping to the beat.
I hop and bounce, I somersault,
And land back on my feet.

I samba, stomp and jitterbug,
I mambo, jig and spin,
When Grandpa gets to fiddling
And plays his violin.

I Chased a Butterfly

Marianne Bluger

I chased a butterfly
She landed on a stone
and I caught her

                   then
I opened my fingers up
and she was gone...

Off among some flowers
coloured orange as she was
and I could not see her
not anywhere there...

Till up she flew
straight towards the sun
it nearly made me blind
and again
she was gone.

O I chased that butterfly
everywhere she went
I chased that butterfly
so perfect and so delicate.

I chased that butterfly
one whole day
but it's all right with me
that she got away.

Cloud Watching

P.K. Page

I saw it too—
a cloud like a man
the man like a snail
the snail like a stone
the stone like a sail
the sail like a bone
the bone like a man.
Catch as catch can.
I saw it too.

MILFORD—the—TURTLE & ME

Patrick Lane

Milford, are there monsters in water,
Down in the weeds and the rocks?
I'd like to meet up with a monster
And hear what it says when it talks.

There are monsters, says Milford quite slowly.
I knew some when I was first small.
Some live down under water.
Some are short, some are fat, some are tall.

I have a good friend who's a monster.
She is kindly and really quite old.
She lives in a big yellow tulip.
She's always been friendly I'm told.

The spiders weave all of her blankets
And she sits in a red carrot chair.
I like her a lot, says small Milford.
As far as I know she's still there.

We walk a long way to the tulips,
Way down to the end of the yard.
At last we get down to the flowers.
By then we are both very tired.

I knock on the tulip quite gently.
A tulip-house is very small!
A voice says, I'm glad you could visit.
I'm glad you could come for a call.

Then out of the tulip comes Mavis.
She's blue from her nose to her knees.
On her feet she wears bright orange slippers.
Her hair is as green as the trees.

She changes shape every few minutes.
Her voice is a high and a low.
She laughs like the colour of roses,
And her eyes are two tiny rainbows.

I sit with small Milford and Mavis,
Not wanting to wander about.
At first she is hidden and quiet,
But after a time she comes out.

We talk about climbing up mountains
And living down under the sea
And why everyone hated monsters,
When monsters are nice as can be.

Most monsters are really quite tiny,
Says Mavis to Milford and me.
My sister's the size of an apple
And my brother's as small as a pea.

You shouldn't be frightened by monsters.
They're really nice people to meet.
Then she offers us butterfly pancakes
With bumblebee butter and beets.

I know now that monsters aren't scary.
I know they're as nice as can be.
Like dragonflies, turtles, and sparrows.
They're friendly like you and like me.

My Ice Cream Cone

Jocelyn Shipley

round
lick lick
cool
drip drip
melt
lick lick
down
drip drip

on my chin
lick
on my chair
drip
slip lick ping
slop drip ping
every lick where

drip
on the floor
stick
in my hair
ick

my ice cream
lick
cone drip my
ice cream cone is
lick
my ice cream cone is
lick
lick
all gone

Dallin's Pool

Angie M. Jansen

I lie on my sunburnt back
In the lukewarm water
The chlorine colouring my
Honey blond hair
Every time a wasp flies by
We yelp like pups
Plunge our heads under
Kid pee
Pool water
We put on old
Grandma bathing suits
Play mermaids
And underwater tea party
Make up pool commercials
Hang out to dry on the poolside swing
Sharks in the shallow end
Dead bugs by the edge

'Tis the Season

Gerry O'Brien

You can serve me turnip at every meal
Or lock me in the shed.
Take away my brand new bike,
Or send me off to bed.
Disconnect the T.V.,
Shave off all my hair.
Make me kiss Aunt Ethel,
Tie me in a chair.
I'll clean my room three times a day,
I'll flush whenever I go.
You'll never have to "speak" to me,
I'll keep the music low.
I'll tell the truth
And never lie.
Cross my heart,
And hope to die.
I'll cover my mouth,
And I won't burp.
I'll drink through a straw
So I don't slurp.

You can sell my dog,
My cat and my fish.
You can even sell me,
If that's what you wish.
But please, oh please, oh please,
OH PLEEEASE!
Don't give me clothes for Christmas.

I Want to Be a Painter

Ken Ward

i want to be a painter
that's what the baker said
i'm tired of baking birthday cakes
and eating gingerbread
i want to paint a picture
as large as a house
with a hundred dancing kangaroos
and one blue waltzing mouse

i want to be a baker
that's what the painter said
i'm tired of painting pictures
while standing on my head
i want to bake an angel cake
a peanut-butter pie
i want to bake a thousand tarts
and toss them in the sky

BUNDLE UP

Susan Ioannou

On winter days
houses wear white hats
and bundle up to their porches in banks
so thick, so deep
sidewalks disappear.

Even an apple tree by the road
has pulled its long johns on.
The street is a white cloak
to cosy the sleeping cars.

On winter days
we bundle up too
and tumble into the snow.
We lie on our backs,
fan angel wings,
and catch white stars on our tongues.

But we're so fat
in red hats and mittens,
black boots, thick ear muffs, wool scarves
nobody trudging along the road
knows any more who we are.

ONLY at NIGHT

Lynn Davies

Be glad you're in bed on the cold
clear nights when I show up.

I seek valleys and low-lying areas
first but you'd never catch me.

I have no body so imagine
me as a humungous white

night-bird flying close to the ground.
My shadow silvers grass and bushes

and rocks. Kills gardens. Freezes
puddles. I'm snow's forerunner.

What am I?

A Song For Sara

Ann Walsh

Sara is serious, strong and secure;
Sara skips, Sara sings, Sara sighs.
Sara swims swiftly, Sara speaks softly,
Sara's smile shines in her eyes.

The Prairie Is Where the Sky Begins

Anne Slade and Doris Bircham

The prairie is where
       the sky begins,
the prairie is home
       to the restless winds.

       Can you taste the prairie
              when it's saskatoon sweet?
       Can you feel the warmth
              of ripening wheat?

       Can you smell wild roses?
              Their scent rides the breeze
       while poplar leaves dance
              high up in the trees.

       Can you find cactus berries
              as summer begins,
       feel prickly pear juice
              trickle down your chin?

Can you dream prairie skies,
    make cloud shapes unfold
as bright sunset flames
    edge hilltops in gold?

Can you catch the wind
    when it tangles your hair,
or chase dust devils
    twirling fast through the air?

Can you follow deer trails
    where the coulee bends,
gather golden leaves
    before autumn ends?

Can you hear the snow
    when it crunches and squeaks,
feel the northwest wind
    nip your nose and your cheeks?

Can you see winter sparkle
    with diamonds aglow?
Can you make white angels
    in fresh-fallen snow?

Can you hear the rustle
        when Northern Lights
waltz across the sky
        on star-sequined nights?

Can you see hillsides
        dressed in mauve and gray
where downy soft crocuses
        nod and sway?

Can you spot meadowlarks,
        black ties at their throats,
welcoming spring
        with each musical note?

Can you wade in the creek
        while it tickles your toes?
Can you feel the freckles
        pop out on your nose?

The prairie is where
        the sky begins,
the prairie is home
        to the restless winds.

Trapeze Artist

Ellen S. Jaffe

One

      leap

        trapeze

          swings

            wide

              space

                rushes in

              free-floating

            air-borne

          I

      wonder

    must I

land?

ELEGY 31 (FLiGHt 111)

rob mclennan

ladies & gentlemen

a groove worn into the air
between calgary & vancouver

you cant take back
sound

Steve

Dani Couture

There's a Viking in my closet—
all three hundred pounds of him
hulked down into the corner.
He's sitting on my very best
black patent leather platforms.
There's a Viking in my closet
and no one believes me.
They say there's no such thing as a Viking,
but clearly they haven't met Steve.
Steve the Viking lost his longboat
and his desire to loot. Now he's sleeping
in my closet, his pillow is my winter boot.

Cleaning My Room

William New

My room is clean!!—I've put away
the action figures, the modelling clay—

I've stuck the games behind the door,
and stacked the puzzles on the floor—

I've parked the cars, I've shelved the books,
I've hung my jacket near the hooks,

and piled the animals on the bed—
I'm not sure where I'll put my head

or hide the heap of railway track—
but I'll figure that out when I come back—

"My room is clean," I shout to Mum
as I run out to play in the sun—

AUTHOR BIOS

Marianne Bluger

Marianne Bluger of Ottawa has written nine books of poetry. She has won the Lampman and numerous other awards. She is a lyric poet also well known for her work in Japanese forms. Her most recent collection is *Early Evening Pieces* and her next, *Zen Mercies/Small Satories*, will be published in spring 2005.

Beverley Brenna

Beverley Brenna M.Ed. is a special education teacher and the author of several books for children, *Daddy Longlegs at Birch Lane, Spider Summer* and *The Keeper of the Trees*. Her new YA title, *Wild Orchid*, is to be published in the fall of 2005. She lives in Saskatoon, SK.

Dani Couture

Dani Couture is a Toronto writer. She is a staff writer for *The Danforth Review* and for *WORD*. Her poetry has appeared in *The Fiddlehead, Taddle Creek, The Windsor ReView, Qwerty* and *Generation*. Dani's first chapbook, *midnight grocery*, was published in 2004 by believe your own press.

Lynn Davies

Lynn Davies' short stories and poems for children have been published in many anthologies. Her first collection of poems, *The Bridge That Carries the Road*, (for adults), was shortlisted for the Gerald Lampert Award and a Governor General's Award in 1999. She works as a private tutor for children with reading difficulties and also conducts creative writing and book making workshops for children in schools and art galleries.

Diane Dawber

Diane Dawber is the author of seven books: *Cankerville, Oatmeal Mittens, My Underwear's Inside Out, How Do You Wrestle a Goldfish, Lifting the Bull, Reading to Heal* and *My Cake's On Fire!* She has recently been honoured in *Poetry Goes to School* as one of the most popular poets for children in the world. She is just completing two new works, *Looking for Snowfleas* for children and *Body, Mind and Image: Landscape as the Poet's Future* for adults. She lives and writes near Amherstview, ON.

Vicki Goodfellow Duke

Vicki Goodfellow Duke lives in Calgary where she teaches public speaking and the oral interpretation of poetry and literature to children. Her poetry has appeared in *CV2, Circle Magazine, Pine Magazine* and numerous anthologies. She was the first place winner of the 2005 Ray Burrell Award, as well as the runner-up for the 2005 Shadow Poetry Chapbook Award.

Susan Ioannou

Susan Ioannou has published hundreds of poems, stories and articles in literary magazines across the country. Her most recent books are the poetry collections *Clarity Between Clouds, Where the Light Waits* and *Coming Home*, the young people's novel *A Real Farm Girl*, and the literary study *A Magical Clockwork: The Art of Writing the Poem*.

Ellen S. Jaffe

Ellen S. Jaffe grew up in New York City and has lived in Ontario, Canada since 1979. She received awards from Arts Hamilton for her poetry collection *Water Children*, and for her book *Writing Your Way: Creating a Personal Journal*. She has also published in journals and anthologies, and written a play for children. A novel for young adults is planned for publication in 2006. Ellen teaches writing workshops, and works in schools with "Learning Through the Arts™."

Angie M. Jansen

Angie M. Jansen's love of writing began at the age of six, with the discovery of reading and writing. She wrote her first hardcover book at age seven entitled *I like you*. Now 20-some years later Angie is just as passionate about writing. She has had several pieces published in Canadian magazines, including *BirthIssues* (Edmonton, AB), and *Poetry Canada* (Ontario, Canada). Angie lives in Edmonton with her husband and two children, working as a lab technician. In what little time she has left over, she can be found scribbling away in many of her writing books.

Patrick Lane

Award-winning poet Patrick Lane has published twenty-one volumes of poetry over the past thirty years. Significant recent titles are: *Poems, New & Selected, The Measure, Old Mother, A Linen Crow, A Caftan Magpie, Selected Poems, Milford & Me*, a collection of children's poems, *Winter* and *Mortal Remains*. His most recent book is *There Is A Season, A Memoir In A Garden*. He lives in Saanichton, BC. His website is *www.patricklane.ca*.

Alison Lohans

Alison Lohans has published thirteen books for children and young adults, including *Waiting for the Sun, Mystery of the Lunchbox Criminal, Nathaniel's Violin* and *Foghorn Passage*. She has won several awards for her writing, and served as Writer-in-Residence at Regina Public Library in 2002-2003. Alison's fourteenth book, *The Raspberry Room*, will be published in 2006. She lives in Regina, SK.

rob mclennan

rob mclennan is the author of ten poetry collections, most recently *what's left* and *stone, book one*. He has a number of chapbooks forthcoming, including *fourteen hearts: a grist* and *corrective lenses*. The editor/publisher of above/ground press and the longpoem magazine *STANZAS*, he edits the cauldron books series through Broken Jaw Press, and, most recently, the anthologies *evergreen: six new poets, side/lines: a new canadian poetics* and *GROUNDSWELL: the best of above/ground press, 1993–2003*. He currently lives in Ottawa, where he co-ordinates events and the semi-annual ottawa small press book fair. With Ottawa poet Stephen Brockwell, he edits *Poetics.ca*.

William New

William New has written several books of poetry and commentaries on Canadian writing. His books for children include *Vanilla Gorilla, Llamas in the Laundry* and *Dream Helmet* (all illustrated by Vivian Bevis). William New lives in Vancouver, BC.

Gerry O'Brien

Gerry O'Brien writes humorous chapter books, picture books, poems and plays for the 7-12 year olds he has been teaching for the past 20 years. As well, Gerry has cowritten three songs for Nelvana Productions in Toronto, one of which will be sung by Funshine Bear in the movie *Care Bears: Journey to Joke-a-lot*. He lives in Argyle Shore, PEI with his wife Loretto and his son Ben.

P.K. Page

P.K. Page is one of this country's outstanding writers and poets. She has published over 20 books and long been recognized internationally. Among her awards are: six honorary doctorates; Officer of the

Order of Canada, 1977; Companion of the Order of Canada, 1999; and the Queen's Golden Jubilee Medal, 2002. In 2004, she was also the recipient of the Terasen Lifetime Achievement Award for an Outstanding Literary Career in British Columbia and the Lieutenant-Governor's Award for Literary Excellence at the BC Book Prizes.

Robin Patterson

Robin Patterson is a writer and artist from Brossard, QC. She has published children's poetry in *Humpty Dumpty* and *Wee Ones* magazines, and was chosen as one of twelve finalists in the 2003 Writers' Union of Canada Writing for Children competition. She also writes poetry and fiction for adults.

Linda Rogers

Writer, teacher and performer Linda Rogers writes poetry, songs and novels for children and adults, always with a concern for the lives of children, who are the most important resource on the planet. With her husband, virtuoso blues mandolinist Rick van Krugel, she sometimes performs *Brown Bag Blues*, a wacky serious musical show for kids of all ages. Her most recent book is *Friday Water*, a novel.

Allan Serafino

Allan Serafino has published three collections of poetry, *Troubled Dreams*, *Alien States* and *Another Way*. His first novel for young adults, *Blood Jaguar*, was published in e-book format in May, 2002, and in soft cover, April, 2003. *Seven Words for Sand* is his most recent book. He lives in Calgary, AB. His website is *www.allanserafino.com*.

Jocelyn Shipley

Jocelyn Shipley's books include a YA novel, *Getting a Life*, and a collection of linked YA stories, *Cross My Heart*, as well as the bestselling *Making Your Own Traditions* craft/cookbooks for families. After spending many years in Toronto and Newmarket, she now lives in Glenburnie, just north of Kingston, ON. Her website is *www.jocelynshipley.com*.

Anne Slade and Doris Bircham

Anne Slade and Doris Bircham ranch with their husbands and families in the Cypress Hills area of southwestern Saskatchewan. They write poetry for children and adults, conduct workshops in schools and entertain at Cowboy Poetry Gatherings and community functions. They have co-authored three books of poetry for young children. Their work has appeared in Canadian and American magazines and anthologies and has been aired on radio and television. They have both been featured on a video *Cowboy Poetry: Words to Live By* by Mediatalk Productions.

Ann Walsh

Ann Walsh is the author of six novels, many of them set during the B.C. Gold Rush. She is also the editor of two anthologies of short stories of historical fiction and the author of a book of poetry. Her latest book, *By the Skin of His Teeth*, the third of her popular Barkerville Mystery series, has just been released.

Ken Ward

Ken Ward is a well-known author and artist. His books include *Mrs. Kitchen's Cats* and *Twelve Kids, One Cow*. His artwork hangs in the Nova Scotia Art Bank and in many private collections. For the past two years he has taught classes in art and writing to children and adults through his studio, Blue Moon Arts. He lives in Halifax, NS.

Irene N. Watts

In 1968 Irene N. Watts came to Canada from Britain, where she had arrived thirty years earlier from Germany, via Kindertransport. She is a writer/playwright and educator. Her trilogy about the children of the Kindertransport (*Good-bye Marianne, Remember Me* and *Finding Sophie*) has been critically acclaimed, and has garnered many awards: the Geoffrey Bilson Award for Historical Fiction for Young People, The Isaac Frischwasser Memorial prize, and Toronto Book Awards in 1999 and 2001. In 2004, *Tapestry of Hope* was honoured with the Yad Vashem Award for Holocaust Studies. Her most recent publication is *A Telling Time*, illustrated by Kathryn E. Shoemaker. She lives and writes in Vancouver, BC.

Patience Wheatley

Patience Wheatley's most recent collection of poetry, *The Astrologer's Daughter*, was published by Pendass Productions in 2004 and launched at the AGM of the League of Canadian Poets in Montreal. She has two other collections published by Goose Lane Editions, as well as many short stories and poetry pubished in Canadian literary magazines. She spent most of her life in Montreal, but now lives in Kingston, ON.

Beryl Young

Beryl Young writes poems and stories, and her children's novel *Wishing Star Summer* was published in 2001. She says you have to have a good reason to write your first book when you are 66 and she did! Beryl lives near the sea in Vancouver and has four grandchildren who give her ideas for writing.